*Dedicated to Saraswati, who fires billions of neurons in my brain in trillions of ways, enabling my mind and body to serve.*

*I offer my deepest gratitude to my ancestors, beginning with Sage Vasishtha and his wife Devi Arundhati, and the legacy of this lineage that instills in me a sense of humility and responsibility. I honor my ancestors by adopting his name as my pen name.*

*I am eternally grateful to my parents, Smt. Suhasini Dubey and Shri Umanath Dubey, for their sacrifices that helped me with my education, values, and opportunities.*

*My heartfelt gratitude also goes to my in-laws, Smt. Uma Aryal and Dr. Kishor Babu Aryal who have been nothing less than my parents for over 20 years. Their guidance, unwavering support, and love have enriched my life in countless ways.*

# CONTENTS

# INTRODUCTION

Throughout human history, the celestial bodies have inspired awe, reverence, and deep curiosity. The nine planets, known as the ***Navagrahas*** in Vedic astrology, are not just astronomical entities but powerful forces that shape our lives, personalities, and destinies. Traditionally, one would think of them as gods or deities and try to please them with flowers and praises. Unfortunately, in the current times, that may not be enough. We need to understand the essence of each of these entities and what aspects of our lives they influence. It should be understood that their energies are profound, influencing every aspect of our existence, from our emotions to our opportunities and challenges. Recognizing, understanding, and harmonizing these energies can lead to greater balance, empowerment, and fulfillment.

This book is a guide which offers options to help you connect with the energies of the Navagrahas in a way that resonates with your personal preferences and spiritual inclinations. Whether you are drawn to traditional Sanskrit mantras, intrigued by the mystical symbolism of seed syllables (*Beeja Mantras*), or inspired by modern poetry, this book offers you multiple pathways to align with the cosmic forces within and around you.

# Disclaimer

*This book does not promote blind faith, superstition, black magic, or any practices that compromise rational thinking or individual well-being.*

*The author does not endorse or recommend visiting unskilled or unqualified astrologers or mystics. On the contrary, the narrative actively emphasizes personal reflection, critical thinking, and responsible decision-making as pathways to growth and clarity.*

*Astrology, like human beings, is complex. No single planet or constellation can define an individual's personality, fate or journey. Readers are encouraged to approach the concepts and ideas presented in this book with an open mind, balanced skepticism, and a focus on their personal journey of self-awareness and self-improvement.*

# WHAT TO EXPECT IN THIS BOOK

### 1. The Navagraha Stotra Mantras

The book begins with a compilation of the ***Navagraha Stotra Mantras,*** powerful hymns of praise and devotion to the nine planets. These Sanskrit verses, steeped in ancient wisdom, vividly describe the qualities, attributes, and energies of each planet. Reciting these mantras not only invokes the blessings of the planets but also connects you to the rich heritage of Vedic spirituality.

### 2. The Beeja Mantras

Next, we delve into the ***Beeja Mantras*** (the seed syllables) that encapsulate the essence of each planet. These timeless mantras are shorter, yet potent, carrying the vibrational frequency of the planets they represent. Their simplicity and power make them accessible for those seeking a focused and meditative practice.

### 3. Modern Relatable Poems for the Navagrahas

Understanding that not everyone feels comfortable with Sanskrit chants or resonates with their traditional structure, this book also offers a contemporary alternative. For each planet, you will find an original modern poem that captures the essence of its energy, qualities, and influence. These poems are crafted to be empowering, relatable, and deeply resonant, enabling you to harness the planetary energies in a way that feels personal and meaningful. With each of the poems, a mindmap has been provided to get a quick glances of characteristics and values of each of the planets.

Besides, the above, a very important aspect of aligning words and vibrations with 'deeds' has been highlighted in the book. Accordingly, a set of Karmic actions befitting the vibrations of each of the planets has been recommended. Performing these actions shall help in maximising the benefits of the chantings and poems.

# PURPOSE OF THE BOOK

This book is not just a collection of ancient verses or modern poetry—it is an invitation to the readers to empower themselves through understanding of the interplay between the cosmic and the personal. The Navagrahas are universal forces, yet their influence is deeply individual.

Planets are not gods or demons intending to destabilise your lives. They are energies, which are just there. There is a cosmic programming and a default setting at the time of your birth. You can use the power of your will and work on your strengths and weaknesses to learn the lessons which you were programmed to learn in this birth.

By providing multiple options—whether through the rhythmic recitation of Sanskrit, the meditative repetition of Beeja sounds, or the emotional resonance of modern poetry—this book allows you to choose the form that best aligns with your beliefs, preferences, and spiritual journey.

# HOW TO USE THIS BOOK

1. **Explore the Navagraha Stotra Mantras**: Discover the traditional hymns and their meanings, immersing yourself in their timeless wisdom.
2. **Meditate on the Beeja Mantras**: Focus on the seed syllables for a powerful vibrational connection to the planets.
3. **Reflect on the Modern Poems**: Engage with contemporary expressions of planetary energies, using them as affirmations, meditative tools, or sources of inspiration.
4. **Choose Your Path**: Feel free to experiment and integrate the practices that resonate most with you. This book is a tool for empowerment, not prescription.

# GENERIC CHANTING PROCEDURE:

Chanting the **Navagraha Mantras** is a powerful way to align yourself with the energies of the nine celestial bodies in Vedic astrology. Each planet governs specific qualities and aspects of life. Here's a detailed guide on **when**, **how**, and **how many times** to chant these mantras.

General Guidelines for Chanting Navagraha Mantras

1. **Timing:**
   Best to take advise from an expert vedic astrologer on when and how many times to chant as per your birth chart. Alternatively, these mantras can be chanted in the early morning during Brahma Muhurta ( 48-96 minutes before sunrise at your location).
   - Alternatively, chant during the planet's **hora** (hour) or day:
     - Sunday: Sun (Surya)
     - Monday: Moon (Chandra)
     - Tuesday: Mars (Mangal), Ketu
     - Wednesday: Mercury (Budha)
     - Thursday: Jupiter (Guru)
     - Friday: Venus (Shukra)
     - Saturday: Saturn (Shani) and Ketu.

2. **Environment:**
   - Choose a clean, quiet, and sacred space.
   - Light a diya (lamp) and incense to purify the

space and invite positive vibrations.
    - Use a mat to sit on
3. **Preparation:**
    - Face east or north while chanting.
    - Take a bath or cleanse yourself before chanting.
    - Wear clean clothes, preferably light or the colours of the specific planet
4. **Chanting Rules:**
    - Chant with devotion and focus on the specific characteristics and values associated with the planet (described later in the book)
    - Maintain a steady pace and clear pronunciation. Quality matters more than quantity.

---

Number of Times to Chant Each Mantra:

For general practice, chanting each mantra **108 times** in each sitting or in multiples of 108, for 42 days is highly effective.

---

Benefits of Chanting Navagraha Mantras

1. **Sun (Surya):** Boosts confidence, leadership, and health.
2. **Moon (Chandra):** Enhances emotional stability, intuition, and peace.
3. **Mars (Mangal):** Increases energy, courage, and determination.
4. **Mercury (Budha):** Improves intellect,

communication, and adaptability.

5. **Jupiter (Guru):** Brings wisdom, spiritual growth, and prosperity.
6. **Venus (Shukra):** Promotes love, creativity, and luxury.
7. **Saturn (Shani):** Teaches discipline, patience, and karmic balance.
8. **Rahu:** Provides worldly success and unconventional wisdom.
9. **Ketu:** Aids in spiritual liberation and detachment.

## A Journey Into Cosmic Alignment

Each mantra and each poem is a step closer to understanding the planetary forces that influence your life and how you can harmonize with them. The Navagrahas are not distant deities or abstract concepts—they are living energies within you, around you, and this book is a guide to harnessing their potential.

Whether you chant, hum, or simply read with intention, this book offers a pathway to align with the cosmos and bring balance, strength, and clarity into your life. Let this be your journey into the profound yet accessible wisdom of the Navagrahas. The choice of how you connect is yours; the cosmic energies are always present, ready to uplift and guide you.

# THE MANTRAS FOR 9 PLANETS

(Navagraha Stotram by Sage Vyasa)

## 1. Sun (Surya)

Devanagari Script:

जपाकुसुमसङ्काशं काश्यपेयं महाद्युतिम्।
तमोऽरिं सर्वपापघ्नं प्रणतोऽस्मि दिवाकरम्।।

**English Transliteration:**
Japakusuma Sankasham Kashyapeyam Mahadyutim
Tamorim Sarva Papaghnam Pranatosmi Divakaram

Meaning:
I bow to the Sun, who is like the red hibiscus flower in radiance, born of Sage Kashyapa, possessing immense brilliance, destroyer of darkness and sins, and the one who makes the day.

---

## 2. Moon (Chandra)

Devanagari Script:

दधिशङ्खतुषाराभं क्षीरोदार्णवसम्भवम्।

नमामि शशिनं सोमं शम्भोर्मुकुटभूषणम्।।

**English Transliteration:**
Dadhi Shankha Tusharabham Ksheerodarnava Sambhavam
Namami Shashinam Somam Shambor Mukuta Bhushanam

Meaning:
I bow to the Moon, who has the white colour and characteristics of curd, conch, and snow, born of the ocean of milk, the one adorned on Shiva's crown, and known as Soma, the distilled one.

---

## 3. Mars (Mangala)

Devanagari Script:

धरणीगर्भसम्भूतं विद्युत्कान्तिसमप्रभम्।
कुमारं शक्तिहस्तं तं मङ्गलं प्रणमाम्यहम्।।

**English Transliteration:**
Dharani Garbha Sambhutam Vidyut Kanti Samaprabham
Kumaram Shakti Hastam Tam
Mangalam Pranamamyaham

Meaning:
I bow to Mars, born of the Earth's womb, shining with the brilliance of lightning, holding a spear in his hand, and known as Mangala, the auspicious one.

---

## 4. Mercury (Budha)

Devanagari Script:

प्रियङ्गुकलिकाश्यामं रूपेणाप्रतिमं बुधम्।
सौम्यं सौम्यगुणोपेतं तं बुधं प्रणमाम्यहम्।।

**English Transliteration:**
Priyangukalika Shyamam Rupenapratimam Budham
Saumyam Saumyagunopetam Tam
Budham Pranamamyaham

Meaning:
I bow to Mercury, the dark-hued like the Priyangu flower, matchless in beauty and is intelligent, peaceful, and endowed with gentle qualities.

---

## 5. Jupiter (Brihaspati)

Devanagari Script:

देवानां च ऋषीणां च गुरुं काञ्चनसन्निभम्।
बुद्धिभूतं त्रिलोकेशं तं नमामि बृहस्पतिम्।।

**English Transliteration:**
Devanam Cha Rishinam Cha Gurum Kanchana Sannibham
Buddhi Bhootam Trilokesham Tam Namami Brihaspatim

Meaning:
I bow to Jupiter, the teacher of the gods and sages, golden-hued, the embodiment of wisdom and the lord of the three worlds.

---

## 6. Venus (Shukra)

Devanagari Script:

हिमकुन्दमृणालाभं दैत्यानां परमं गुरुम्।
सर्वशास्त्रप्रवक्तारं भार्गवं प्रणमाम्यहम्।।

**English Transliteration:**
Himakunda Mrinalabham Daityanam Paramam Gurum
Sarva Shastra Pravaktaram Bhargavam Pranamamyaham

Meaning:
I bow to Venus, white like the jasmine flower and the lotus stem, the great teacher of demons, the expert in all scriptures, and the son of Sage Bhrigu.

---

## 7. Saturn (Shani)

Devanagari Script:

नीलाञ्जनसमाभासं रविपुत्रं यमाग्रजम्।
छायामार्तण्डसम्भूतं तं नमामि शनैश्चरम्।।

**English Transliteration:**
Nilanjana Samabhasam Raviputram Yamagrajam
Chhaya Martanda Sambhutam Tam
Namami Shaneshwaram

Meaning:
I bow to Saturn, dark as blue collyrium,the elder brother of Yama (god of death), the son of the Sun and born of Chhaya (shadow).

## 8. Rahu

Devanagari Script:

अर्धकायं महावीर्यं चन्द्रादित्यविमर्दनम्।
सिंहिकागर्भसम्भूतं तं राहुं प्रणमाम्यहम्।।

**English Transliteration:**
Ardha Kayam Mahaveeryam Chandraditya Vimardanam
Simhika Garbha Sambhutam Tam
Rahum Pranamamyaham

Meaning:
I bow to Rahu, who is half-bodied, full of valour, tormentor of the Sun and Moon, and born of Simhika (lioness).

## 9. Ketu

Devanagari Script:

पलाशपुष्पसङ्काशं तारकाग्रहमस्तकम्।
रौद्रं रौद्रात्मकं घोरं तं केतुं प्रणमाम्यहम्।।

**English Transliteration:**
Palasha Pushpa Sankasham Taraka Graha Mastakam
Roudram Roudratmakam Ghoram Tam
Ketum Pranamamyaham

Meaning:
I bow to Ketu, resembling the Palasha flower
in appearance, the head of the stars and

planets, fierce and terrifying in nature.

---

**Conclusion**

Each mantra, when recited with focus and devotion, strengthens the connection to the planet's energy, mitigates malefic effects, and enhances beneficial influences. Chanting them with the proper pronunciation (phonetics) and understanding their meaning deepens the practice and spiritual impact.

# BEEJA MANTRAS OF NINE PLANETS

**Beeja Mantras** (seed mantras) of nine planets (*Navagrahas*) are concise, powerful invocations that encapsulate the core energy of each planet in a few syllables.

---

## 1. Sun (Surya)

**Devanagari Script:**

ॐ ह्रां ह्रीं ह्रौं सः सूर्याय नमः।

**Transliteration:**
**Om Hraam Hreem Hroum Sah Suryaya Namah**

**Effects of the Sound Vibrations:**
**Hraam**: Vibration linked to vitality and willpower; it invokes the Sun's fiery, life-sustaining energy.

**Hreem**: Associated with illumination and divine consciousness, often used in contexts of spiritual awakening.

**Hroum**: Resonates with transformation and removal of ignorance, aligning well with the Sun's role as the dispeller of darkness.

**Meaning:**
I bow to the Sun, the source of vitality, power, and light, invoking its energy for strength and illumination.

---

## 2. Moon (Chandra)

**Devanagari Script:**

ॐ श्रां श्रीं श्रौं सः चन्द्राय नमः।

**Transliteration:**
**Om Shraam Shreem Shroum Sah Chandraya Namah**

**Effects of the Sound Vibrations:**

**Shraam**: Represents grounding and emotional balance, a valid interpretation tied to the Moon's nurturing energy.

**Shreem**: Associated with abundance, peace, and prosperity, as it's widely used in mantras for Lakshmi and feminine energies.

**Shroum**: Balances the mind, resonating with the Moon's influence over the psyche and emotions.

**Meaning:**
I bow to the Moon, the nurturer of emotions and intuition, invoking its calming and balancing energy.

---

## 3. Mars (Mangala)

**Devanagari Script:**

ॐ क्रां क्रीं क्रौं सः भौमाय नमः।

**Transliteration:**
**Om Kraam Kreem Kroum Sah Bhaumaya Namah**

**Effects of the Sound Vibrations:**

**Kraam:** Associated with courage and action, which denotes Mars' fiery and assertive qualities.

**Kreem:** Transformation and destruction of negativity are valid meanings, often tied to Mars' aggressive energy.

**Kroum:** Energetic power to overcome obstacles aligned with Mars' warrior-like nature.

**Meaning:**
I bow to Mars, the planet of courage, energy, and strength, invoking its fiery power to overcome challenges.

---

## 4. Mercury (Budha)

**Devanagari Script:**

ॐ ब्रां ब्रीं ब्रौं सः बुधाय नमः।

**Transliteration:**
**Om Braam Breem Broum Sah Budhaya Namah**

**Effects of the Sound Vibrations:**

**Braam**: Sharpness of intellect and analytical ability which denoted Mercury's domain of intelligence.

**Breem**: Enhancing communication and adaptability is associated with Mercury's influence.

**Broum**: Clarity in reasoning aligned with Mercury's role in logic and expression.

**Meaning:**

I bow to Mercury, the planet of intellect, communication, and wisdom, invoking its energy for clarity and understanding.

---

## 5. Jupiter (Brihaspati)

**Devanagari Script:**

ॐ ग्रां ग्रीं ग्रौं सः गुरवे नमः।

**Transliteration:**
**Om Graam Greem Groum Sah Gurave Namah**

**Interpretations of the Sound Vibrations:**

**Graam**: Expansion and wisdom aligned with Jupiter's expansive, benefic nature.

**Greem**: Spiritual enlightenment denotes Jupiter's role as the teacher of gods and knowledge bearer.

**Groum**: Abundance and blessings which are interpretations for Jupiter's generous energy.

**Meaning:**
I bow to Jupiter, the teacher of the gods and the planet of wisdom, invoking its energy for growth and knowledge.

---

## 6. Venus (Shukra)

**Devanagari Script:**

ॐ द्रां द्रीं द्रौं सः शुक्राय नमः।

**Transliteration:**
**Om Draam Dreem Droum Sah Shukraya Namah**

**Effects of the Sound Vibrations:**

**Draam**: Beauty and refinement which align with Venus' focus on aesthetics and love.

**Dreem**: Harmony, creativity, and attraction which are key attributes of Venus in relationships and pleasures.

**Droum**: Prosperity and luxury which are associated with Venus' energy of wealth and sensuality.

**Meaning:**
I bow to Venus, the planet of beauty, love, and harmony, invoking its energy for creativity and relationships.

---

## 7. Saturn (Shani)

**Devanagari Script:**

ॐ प्रां प्रीं प्रौं सः शनैश्चराय नमः।

**Transliteration:**
**Om Praam Preem Proum Sah Shanaishcharaya Namah**

**Effects of the Sound Vibrations:**

**Praam**: Stability and patience which are reflections of Saturn's grounding energy.

**Preem**: Discipline and focus which indicate Saturn's role in karma and life lessons.

**Proum**: Perseverance and resilience which denote Saturn's enduring nature.

**Meaning:**
I bow to Saturn, the planet of discipline and karmic lessons, invoking its energy for perseverance and patience.

---

## 8. Rahu

**Devanagari Script:**

ॐ भ्रां भ्रीं भ्रौं सः राहवे नमः।

**Transliteration:**
**Om Bhraam Bhreem Bhroum Sah Rahave Namah**

**Effects of the Sound Vibrations:**

**Bhraam**: Ambition and unconventional thinking aligned with Rahu's shadowy and ambitious nature.

**Bhreem**: Transformation and insight which come from Rahu's energy of pushing boundaries.

**Bhroum**: Breaking limitations and seeking higher truths

which resonate with Rahu's mysterious influence.

**Meaning:**
I bow to Rahu, the shadow planet of ambition and transformation, invoking its energy for insights and breakthrough.

---

## 9. Ketu

Devanagari Script:

ॐ स्रां स्रीं स्रौं सः केतवे नमः।

**Transliteration:**
**Om Sraam Sreem Sroum Sah Ketave Namah**

**Effects of the Sound Vibrations:**

**Sraam**: Detachment and introspection aligned with Ketu's spiritual focus.

**Sreem**: Inner clarity and awakening which are tied to Ketu's liberation energy.

**Sroum**: Transcendence and mystical insights which come from Ketu's association with moksha (spiritual liberation).

**Meaning:**
I bow to Ketu, the shadow planet of detachment and spiritual liberation, invoking its energy for inner growth and enlightenment.

# KARMIC MEASURES TO COMBINE WITH THE VOCAL TOOLS

Below is a list of Karmic measures or Acts of Service corresponding to each planet. Performing these acts of service in conjunction with chanting mantras or reciting poems amplifies the transformative effects of planetary remedies. While mantras or the poems which follow, align your vibrational frequency with the planet's energy, acts of service engage you on a karmic level, creating tangible actions that reflect the planet's values.

This holistic approach not only harmonizes the planetary influences in your life but also fosters spiritual growth and balance by aligning your thoughts, words, and deeds with cosmic energies. Together, they create a synergy that enhances the overall results, paving the way for deeper alignment and positive transformation.

## Detailed Acts Of Service For Navagrahas:

1. **Sun (Surya):**

    - **Respect father figures:** Offer support and spend time with your father or paternal figures. Acknowledge their contributions to your life with gratitude.
    - **Honor elders and authority figures:** Actively show respect to elders, leaders, or mentors in your

community. Offer assistance or simply listen to their wisdom.
- **Volunteer in leadership roles:** Take responsibility in social or professional settings, demonstrating integrity and reliability.

2. **Moon (Chandra):**

- **Care for your mother or nurturing figures:** Help your mother or anyone who has played a maternal role in your life by offering emotional support or practical assistance.
- **Provide comfort to others:** Be a source of empathy and understanding for those experiencing emotional distress or instability.
- **Engage in caregiving activities:** Volunteer at shelters, hospitals, or orphanages where nurturing and emotional care are needed.

3. **Mars (Mangal):**

- **Help your siblings:** Support your siblings in their personal or professional challenges, fostering stronger family ties.
- **Engage in acts of bravery:** Stand up for justice or protect those in vulnerable situations. This could be as simple as helping someone in need or as significant as joining a cause for social justice.
- **Channel energy through action:** Participate in physical volunteer work like disaster relief or community-building activities.

4. **Mercury (Budha):**

- **Teach others:** Share your knowledge by tutoring students, helping someone learn a skill, or guiding them in their career or studies.
- **Mentor someone younger:** Offer mentorship to young individuals, especially in areas where you have expertise, helping them develop confidence and abilities.
- **Promote clear communication:** Mediate conflicts or facilitate productive conversations in groups or relationships.

5. **Jupiter (Guru):**

- **Honor your teachers:** Acknowledge and appreciate the guidance of your teachers, gurus, or spiritual mentors. Offer them assistance or gifts as a token of gratitude.
- **Support education initiatives:** Contribute to schools, libraries, or educational programs for underprivileged children.
- **Promote wisdom and knowledge:** Host or attend spiritual discussions, workshops, or religious events to spread and absorb higher learning.

6. **Venus (Shukra):**

- **Support artists:** Help artists or creators in need, whether by providing resources, promoting their work, or offering encouragement.
- **Aid those seeking guidance:** Be a mentor or counselor for individuals navigating personal or creative challenges.
- **Foster beauty and harmony:** Contribute to projects that beautify and uplift environments,

such as community art or gardens.

7. **Saturn (Shani):**
    - **Serve the underprivileged:** Provide food, clothing, or support to laborers, beggars, or anyone facing hardships.
    - **Assist the elderly:** Spend time with elderly individuals, offering companionship or help with daily tasks.
    - **Engage in disciplined work:** Volunteer for activities requiring dedication and patience, such as long-term community service projects.
8. **Rahu:**
    - **Assist individuals struggling with addiction:** Support rehabilitation efforts, whether by volunteering at rehab centers or helping someone personally overcome their struggles.
    - **Aid mental health initiatives:** Spread awareness about mental health issues or offer support to those facing emotional challenges.
    - **Promote unconventional solutions:** Help individuals embrace change by sharing innovative ideas or assisting with their unconventional pursuits.
9. **Ketu:**
    - **Engage in acts of spiritual guidance:** Guide others on spiritual paths by sharing meditation techniques, scripture readings, or inspirational teachings.

- **Support meditation groups:** Facilitate or join meditation, yoga, or mindfulness sessions to create a community of spiritual seekers.
- **Embrace detachment through charity:** Donate anonymously to spiritual or charitable causes, detaching from the need for recognition.

# MODERN DAY POETRY WITH EXPLANATIONS

The celestial bodies (plantets and stars) are not just distant orbs of light; their rhythmic movement and patterns have a rhythm with our lives. Each planet embodies a unique energy—a force that shapes our intellect, emotions, desires, and challenges. In the modern world, these energies remain as influential as ever, but their wisdom can often feel inaccessible, veiled by difficult Sanskrit terms or distant myths.

This chapter aims to bridge that gap by bringing the planets to life through poetry. Here, the timeless essence of the ***Navagrahas*** is reimagined in verses that speak to contemporary hearts and minds. Each poem serves as a mirror, reflecting the planet's gifts, lessons, and challenges in a relatable, modern context. Whether it's the Sun's unyielding confidence, the Moon's nurturing embrace, or Saturn's stern yet transformative lessons, these poems are crafted to inspire readers to connect with these celestial archetypes.

## How To Benefit Most From These Poems

As you read these poems, allow yourself to feel the essence of each planet. Reflect on how its energy shows up in your life and how you can harmonize with it. Use the verses as meditations, affirmations, or even as starting points for your own creative exploration of planetary energies.

Let these poems be your celestial companions, offering both inspiration and introspection as you journey through the cosmos within and around you.

# SUN - THE KING

**Role:** Represents authority, leadership, and vitality.
**Significance:** The Sun is considered the soul (*Atman*) of the universe and signifies willpower, ego, confidence, and one's essence of being.
**Associated Aspects:** Father figure, government, power, health, and self-expression.

Oh Sun, great giver of life and flame,
You call us to rise, to claim our fame.
With rays that cut through darkest of nights,
You guide us toward the path that is right.

Your strength, a fire that will not wane,
Through storms of doubt, through joy and pain.
You teach us courage, bold and true,
To face each day with a clearer view.

Oh master of purpose, shining bright,
Ignite my soul with your guiding light.
Through trials steep and shadows long,
You make me steadfast, fierce, and strong.

With truth as your banner, you lead the way,
To live with honor, come what may.
No fear, no falsehood can ever stay,
When the Sun's pure glow lights my day.

Oh radiant heart, with golden hue,
You remind me to shine in all I do.
Through acts of will, through deeds of grace,
To meet each challenge with a fearless face.

In your warmth, I find my spark,
To blaze a trail through the cold and dark.
With purpose clear and spirit high,
I soar like fire across the sky.

Oh Sun, my guide, my constant flame,
Teach me to honor life's sacred game.
To lead, to love, to shine, to be,
A beacon of light for all to see.

## Explanation

*Oh Sun, great giver of life and flame,*
*You call us to rise, to claim our fame.*
*With rays that cut through darkest of nights,*
*You guide us toward the path that is right.*

This stanza introduces the Sun as the source of life and purpose, inspiring the reader to rise above challenges and claim their identity. It encourages embracing the Sun's illuminating energy to find clarity and direction in life.

*Your strength, a fire that will not wane,*
*Through storms of doubt, through joy and pain.*
*You teach us courage, bold and true,*
*To face each day with a clearer view.*

Here, the Sun's unwavering energy is highlighted, reminding the reader to remain steadfast through life's trials. It emphasizes the importance of courage and resilience, empowering the reader to face each day with renewed determination and perspective.

*Oh master of purpose, shining bright,*
*Ignite my soul with your guiding light.*
*Through trials steep and shadows long,*
*You make me steadfast, fierce, and strong.*

This stanza calls upon the Sun's power to fuel the reader's sense of purpose and inner strength. It inspires the reader to endure life's difficulties with unwavering resolve, trusting in the Sun's guiding energy to overcome obstacles.

*With truth as your banner, you lead the way,*
*To live with honor, come what may.*
*No fear, no falsehood can ever stay,*
*When the Sun's pure glow lights my day.*

Here, the Sun is celebrated as a symbol of truth and integrity. The stanza encourages the reader to live with honor and authenticity, dispelling fear and falsehood by embracing the Sun's illuminating power.

*Oh radiant heart, with golden hue,*
*You remind me to shine in all I do.*
*Through acts of will, through deeds of grace,*
*To meet each challenge with a fearless face.*

This stanza reflects the Sun's role in inspiring self-expression and positivity. It urges the reader to shine brightly in all endeavors, meeting challenges with grace and fearlessness.

*In your warmth, I find my spark,*

*To blaze a trail through the cold and dark.*
*With purpose clear and spirit high,*
*I soar like fire across the sky.*

The Sun's energy is invoked here as a source of inspiration and vitality. The stanza empowers the reader to find their inner spark, take bold action, and pursue their goals with clarity and enthusiasm.

*Oh Sun, my guide, my constant flame,*
*Teach me to honor life's sacred game.*
*To lead, to love, to shine, to be,*
*A beacon of light for all to see.*

In the closing stanza, the Sun is acknowledged as a guide and source of purpose. Since the Sun is the King of the Solar System, it inspires the reader to live with integrity, love, and leadership, becoming a shining example for others and embodying the radiant energy of a father figure.

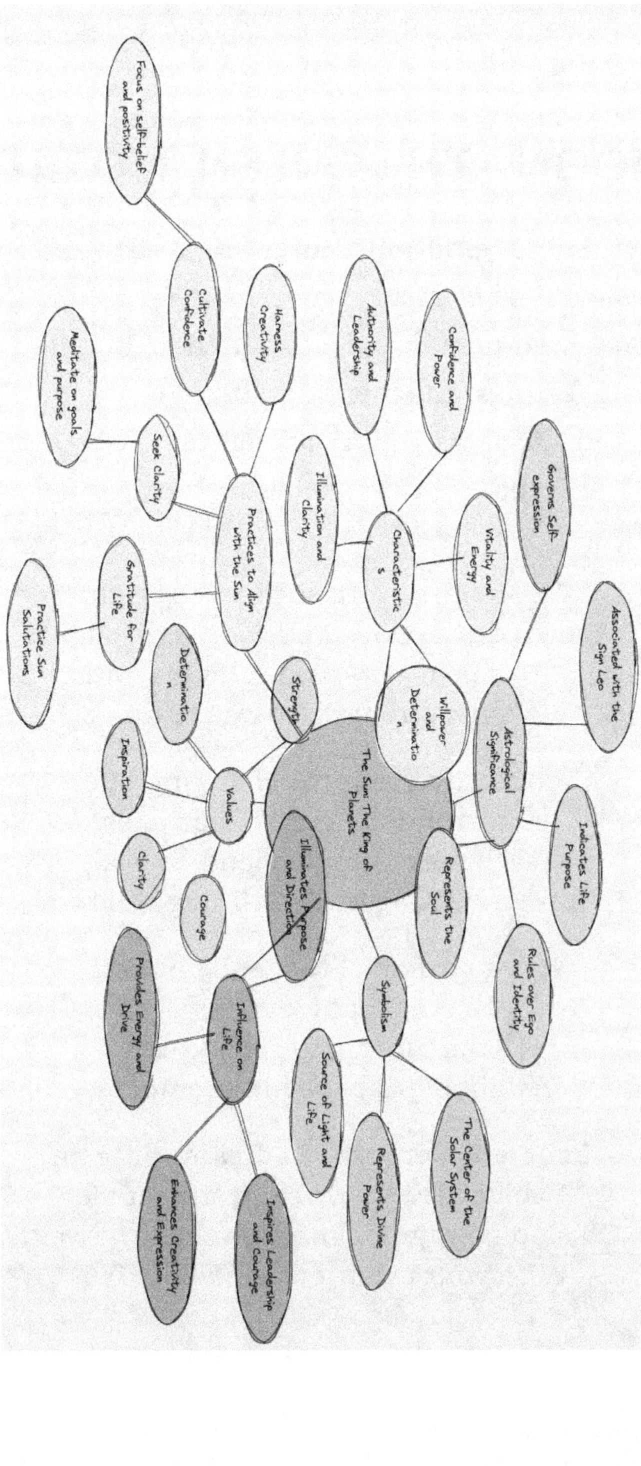
The Sun: The King of Planets
Characteristics
Confidence and Power
Authority and Leadership
Illumination and Clarity
Vitality and Energy
Willpower and Determination
Astrological Significance
Governs Self-expression
Associated with the Sign Leo
Indicates Life Purpose
Rules over Ego and Identity
Represents the Soul
Symbolism
The Center of the Solar System
Represents Divine Power
Source of Light and Life
Illuminates Purpose and Direction
Influence on Life
Inspires Leadership and Courage
Enhances Creativity and Expression
Provides Energy and Drive
Values
Courage
Clarity
Inspiration
Determination
Strength
Practices to Align with the Sun
Gratitude for Life
Practice Sun Salutations
Seek Clarity
Meditate on goals and purpose
Cultivate Confidence
Focus on self-belief and positivity
Harness Creativity

# MOON - THE QUEEN, MOTHER

**Role:** Symbolizes emotions, nurturing, and intuition.

**Significance:** The Moon governs the mind (*Manas*), emotional well-being, and adaptability. It reflects one's inner self, feelings, and mental stability.

**Associated Aspects:** Mother figure, home, comfort, imagination, and emotional relationships.

Oh Moon, so soft, so pure, so bright,
You guide the tides, you soothe the night.
With silken glow, you calm the mind,
A quiet strength, so rare to find.

Your face reflects the changing skies,
A mirror of where my spirit lies.
Teach me to flow, to bend, to heal,
Through shifting truths, through all I feel.

Oh guardian of the tender heart,
You teach the art of love's sweet start.
To nurture all, to give, to care,
A light of peace beyond compare.

Your whispers echo in dreams unseen,
A voice of wisdom, calm and serene.
Oh Moon, my guide through shadow's veil,
With your intuition, I shall not fail.

In fleeting forms, you wax, you wane,
Yet always return, renewed again.
Teach me the beauty of life's own tide,
To embrace each turn, to trust, to abide.

Oh keeper of the creative spark,
You light the way through the deepest dark.
With dreams you gift, with belief you weave,
A path of grace I shall believe.

Oh Moon, so gentle, so strong, so wise,
You hold the truth behind my eyes.
Teach me to see, to trust, to feel,
To nurture the world and let wounds heal.

In your glow, I find my peace,
Through your grace, my burdens cease.
Oh Moon, my heart is one with you,
A beacon of calm, forever true.

## Explanation

*Oh Moon, so soft, so pure, so bright,*
*You guide the tides, you soothe the night.*
*With silken glow, you calm the mind,*
*A quiet strength, so rare to find.*

This stanza introduces the Moon as a calming and nurturing presence. It empowers the reader to embrace the Moon's gentle strength, finding solace and mental clarity in its soothing energy.

*Your face reflects the changing skies,*
*A mirror of where my spirit lies.*

*Teach me to flow, to bend, to heal,*
*Through shifting truths, through all I feel.*

Here, the Moon's phases symbolize life's changes and emotions. The stanza inspires the reader to adapt gracefully to life's ups and downs, fostering resilience and emotional healing by embracing change.

*Oh guardian of the tender heart,*
*You teach the art of love's sweet start.*
*To nurture all, to give, to care,*
*A light of peace beyond compare.*

This stanza highlights the Moon's nurturing qualities, like that of a mother. It encourages the reader to cultivate compassion, care for others, and build meaningful connections, embodying the Moon's peaceful energy.

*Your whispers echo in dreams unseen,*
*A voice of wisdom, calm and serene.*
*Oh Moon, my guide through shadow's veil,*
*With your intuition, I shall not fail.*

The Moon's role as an intuitive guide is celebrated here. It inspires the reader to trust their inner voice and navigate life's uncertainties with confidence and wisdom.

*In fleeting forms, you wax, you wane,*
*Yet always return, renewed again.*
*Teach me the beauty of life's own tide,*
*To embrace each turn, to trust, to abide.*

This stanza reflects the Moon's cyclical nature, teaching the reader to accept life's ebb and flow. It empowers them to find beauty and growth in transitions and trust the process of renewal.

*Oh keeper of the creative spark,*
*You light the way through the deepest dark.*
*With dreams you gift, with belief you weave,*
*A path of grace I shall believe.*

The Moon's connection to creativity and imagination is emphasized here. The stanza encourages the reader to embrace their artistic potential and let belief guide them through challenges.

*Oh Moon, so gentle, so strong, so wise,*
*You hold the truth behind my eyes.*
*Teach me to see, to trust, to feel,*
*To nurture the world and let wounds heal.*

This stanza celebrates the Moon's balance of gentleness and strength. It inspires the reader to look inward for truth, trust their emotions, and use these insights to heal themselves and others.

*In your glow, I find my peace,*
*Through your grace, my burdens cease.*
*Oh Moon, my heart is one with you,*
*A beacon of calm, forever true.*

The closing stanza reflects the Moon's power to bring serenity and unity. It empowers the reader to find peace within themselves and radiate that calm to the world, becoming a source of tranquility and light.

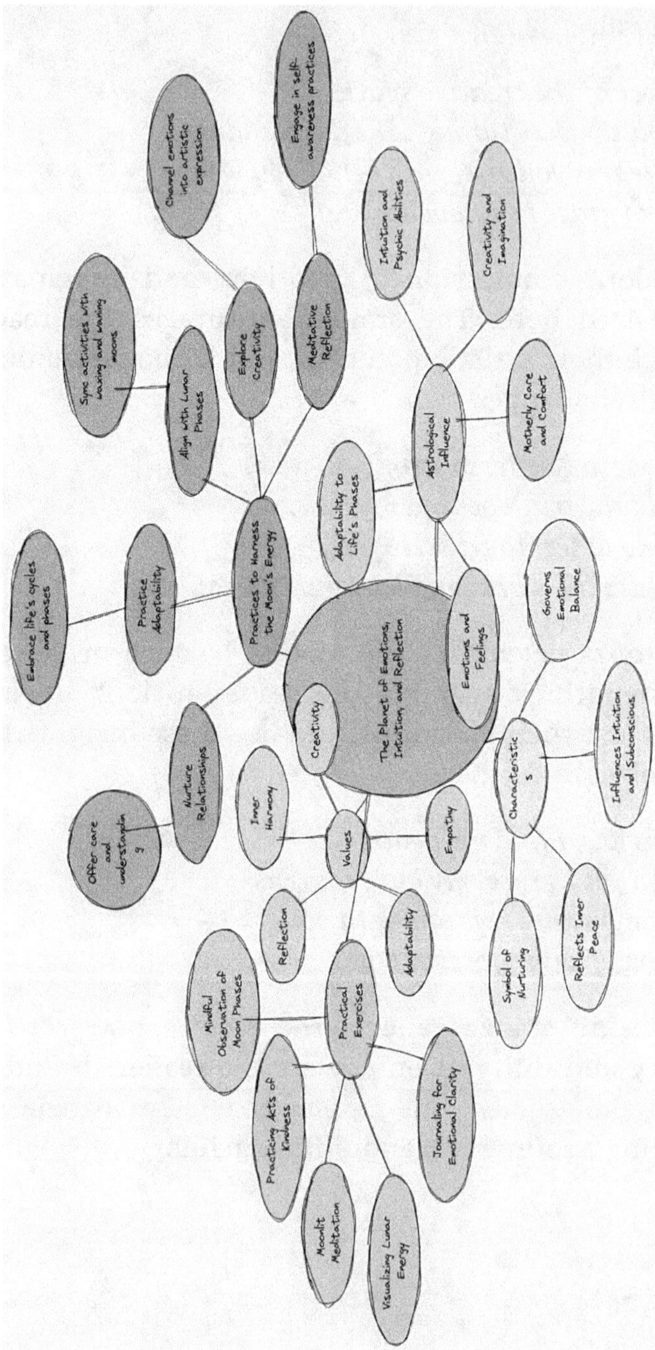
The Planet of Emotions, Intuition, and Reflection
Practices to Harness the Moon's Energy
Align with Lunar Phases
Sync activities with waxing and waning moons
Explore Creativity
Channel emotions into artistic expression
Meditative Reflection
Engage in self-awareness practices
Practice Adaptability
Embrace life's cycles and phases
Nurture Relationships
Offer care and understandin g
Astrological Influence
Intuition and Psychic Abilities
Creativity and Imagination
Motherly Care and Comfort
Adaptability to Life's Phases
Emotions and Feelings
Creativity
Characteristic s
Governs Emotional Balance
Influences Intuition and Subconscious
Reflects Inner Peace
Symbol of Nurturing
Values
Inner Harmony
Empathy
Reflection
Adaptability
Practical Exercises
Mindful Observation of Moon Phases
Practicing Acts of Kindness
Journaling for Emotional Clarity
Moonlit Meditation
Visualizing Lunar Energy

# MARS - THE HEAD OF ARMED FORCES

**Role:** Represents courage, energy, determination.
**Significance:** Mars symbolizes strength, action, ambition, and the ability to overcome obstacles. It also governs discipline and assertiveness.
**Associated Aspects:** Brothers, land, property, competition, and warfare.

Oh Mars, the fire within my soul,
You drive my steps, you make me whole.
With strength unyielding, fierce and true,
You light the path to all I do.

Your energy burns, so bold, so bright,
A warrior's heart, my guiding light.
Through storms of doubt, I will not sway,
For Mars inspires the brave to stay.

Oh guardian force, with spear in hand,
You teach me courage, to take a stand.
No fear can bind, no chains remain,
Through will and grit, I break the strain.

Your flame commands, "Rise up, begin,
The battle's won when you fight within."

Through trials steep, through uphill climb,
I forge my strength, I bide my time.

Oh Mars, the power to protect and guide,
You teach me to stand with honor and pride.
Injustice falls when I speak my truth,
A voice of the righteous, bold from youth.

In action's forge, my will is made,
Through discipline's fire, I'm not afraid.
With every step, with every strive,
I claim the joy of being alive.

Oh Mars, my shield, my inner fire,
You fuel my passion, lift me higher.
To lead, to act, to face the fray,
With Mars as my guide, I seize the day.

## Explanation

*Oh Mars, the fire within my soul,*
*You drive my steps, you make me whole.*
*With strength unyielding, fierce and true,*
*You light the path to all I do.*

This stanza introduces Mars as the source of inner strength and vitality. It empowers the reader to recognize the fiery energy within themselves that drives their actions and helps them navigate life with resilience and purpose.

*Your energy burns, so bold, so bright,*
*A warrior's heart, my guiding light.*
*Through storms of doubt, I will not sway,*

*For Mars inspires the brave to stay.*

Here, Mars is depicted as a beacon of courage and determination. The stanza inspires the reader to hold firm in the face of challenges and doubt, drawing on Mars' unwavering energy to persevere with a warrior's spirit.

*Oh guardian force, with spear in hand,*
*You teach me courage, to take a stand.*
*No fear can bind, no chains remain,*
*Through will and grit, I break the strain.*

This stanza highlights Mars' protective and empowering qualities. It encourages the reader to stand up for themselves and others, breaking free from fear and limitations through sheer willpower and determination.

*Your flame commands, "Rise up, begin,*
*The battle's won when you fight within."*
*Through trials steep, through uphill climb,*
*I forge my strength, I bide my time.*

Mars' energy is framed as a call to action, urging the reader to confront their inner battles with courage and persistence. The stanza emphasizes that true strength is built through enduring trials and staying focused on long-term goals.

*Oh Mars, the power to protect and guide,*
*You teach me to stand with honor and pride.*
*Injustice falls when I speak my truth,*

*A voice of the righteous, bold from youth.*

This stanza reflects Mars' association with righteousness and justice. It inspires the reader to act with integrity, speak their truth boldly, and stand as a force for fairness and moral strength in the world.

*In action's forge, my will is made,*
*Through discipline's fire, I'm not afraid.*
*With every step, with every strive,*
*I claim the joy of being alive.*

Here, Mars' transformative energy is celebrated. The stanza encourages the reader to embrace disciplined effort and take bold steps, finding fulfillment and purpose in their actions and achievements.

*Oh Mars, my shield, my inner fire,*
*You fuel my passion, lift me higher.*
*To lead, to act, to face the fray,*
*With Mars as my guide, I seize the day.*

The closing stanza captures Mars' essence of being the head of the armed forces, as a source of motivation and leadership. It empowers the reader to channel their passion into meaningful actions, leading with courage and determination, and seizing every opportunity to make a difference.

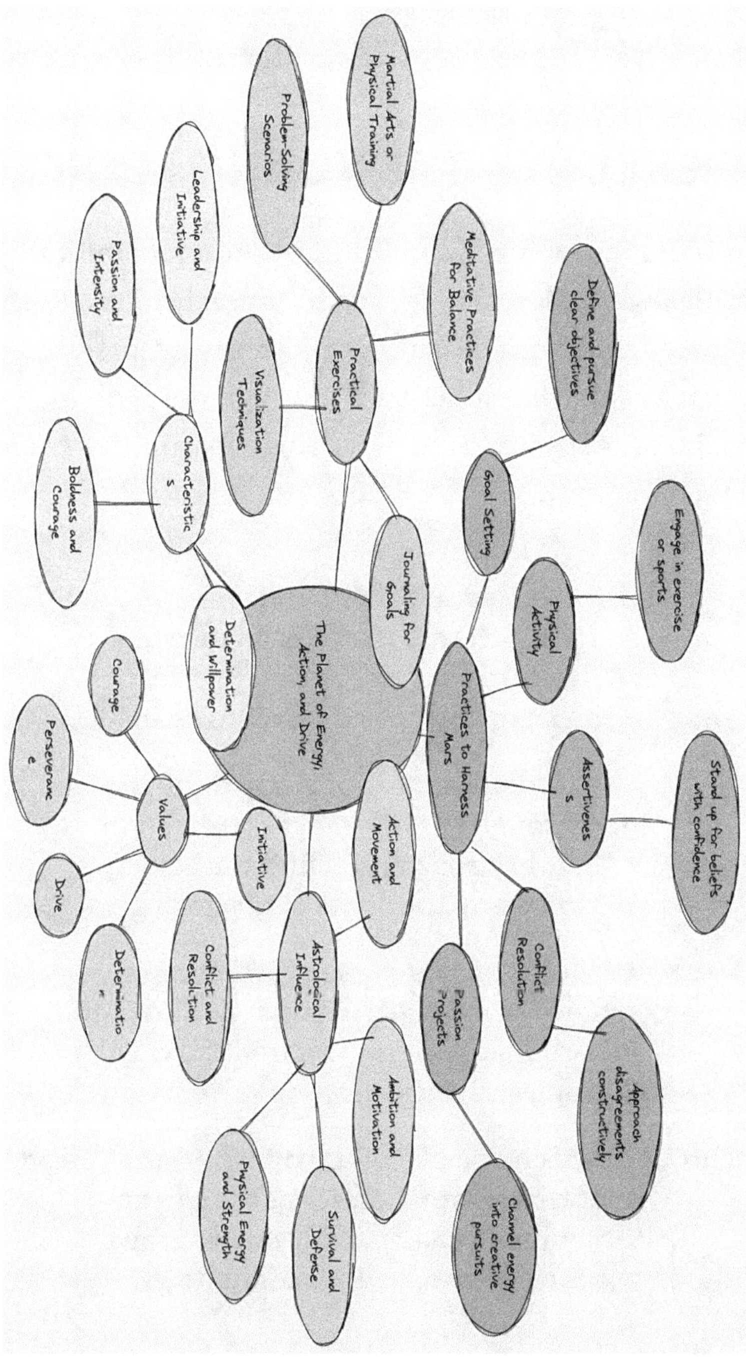
The Planet of Energy, Action, and Drive
Determination and Willpower
Characteristics
Boldness and Courage
Passion and Intensity
Leadership and Initiative
Practical Exercises
Visualization Techniques
Problem-Solving Scenarios
Martial Arts or Physical Training
Meditative Practices for Balance
Journaling for Goals
Goal Setting
Define and pursue clear objectives
Physical Activity
Engage in exercise or sports
Practices to Harness Mars
Assertiveness
Stand up for beliefs with confidence
Conflict Resolution
Approach disagreements constructively
Passion Projects
Channel energy into creative pursuits
Action and Movement
Astrological Influence
Ambition and Motivation
Survival and Defense
Physical Energy and Strength
Conflict and Resolution
Values
Courage
Perseverance
Initiative
Drive
Determination

# MERCURY - THE YOUNG PRINCE

**Role:** Signifies intellect, communication, adaptability.
**Significance:** Mercury governs speech, intelligence, analytical skills, and learning. It also represents business acumen and quick thinking.
**Associated Aspects:** Trade, writing, reasoning, friends, and technology.

Oh Mercury, swift and wise,
You teach the art where brilliance lies.
With words like rivers, flowing clear,
You shape the world for all to hear.

Your mind, a maze of sharp design,
Cuts through the fog, makes truth align.
In every puzzle, you find the key,
Unlocking the doors of mystery.

Oh guide of change, so quick, so sure,
You show the strength in the agile and pure.
Where chaos reigns, you find the way,
Through shifting tides, you never stray.

Through speech and thought, you weave the thread,
A fabric bright where ideas are spread.
With wit and charm, your power grows,
In every word, your wisdom flows.

Oh spark of learning, ever new,
Teach me to seek and see it through.
With curiosity, I'll chart the skies,
And grasp the truths where knowledge lies.

Oh Mercury, grant me the art,
To share my mind and touch the heart.
To adapt, to flex, to stand, to bend,
And find the harmony time will send.

Through you, I'll rise with steady pace,
To meet the world with a nimble grace.
A seeker, a thinker, bold and free,
Oh Mercury, your strength flows through me.

## Explanation

*Oh Mercury, swift and wise,*
*You teach the art where brilliance lies.*
*With words like rivers, flowing clear,*
*You shape the world for all to hear.*

This stanza introduces Mercury as the planet of intelligence and communication, inspiring the reader to embrace clarity in their thoughts and words. It empowers them to use their voice effectively to make an impact and express themselves with confidence.

*Your mind, a maze of sharp design,*
*Cuts through the fog, makes truth align.*
*In every puzzle, you find the key,*
*Unlocking the doors of mystery.*

Here, Mercury's analytical and problem-solving abilities

are celebrated. It encourages the reader to tackle challenges with logic and curiosity, reminding them of their innate ability to discover solutions and uncover deeper truths.

*Oh guide of change, so quick, so sure,*
*You show the strength in the agile and pure.*
*Where chaos reigns, you find the way,*
*Through shifting tides, you never stray.*

This stanza reflects Mercury's adaptability and resilience in the face of change. It inspires the reader to embrace life's uncertainties with agility and confidence, trusting their ability to navigate dynamic situations successfully.

*Through speech and thought, you weave the thread,*
*A fabric bright where ideas are spread.*
*With wit and charm, your power grows,*
*In every word, your wisdom flows.*

Mercury's charm and eloquence are highlighted here, encouraging the reader to use their intellect and communication skills to foster understanding and connection. It reminds them of the power of thoughtful and persuasive expression.

*Oh spark of learning, ever new,*
*Teach me to seek and see it through.*
*With curiosity, I'll chart the skies,*
*And grasp the truths where knowledge lies.*

This stanza celebrates Mercury's role as a seeker of knowledge and growth. It urges the reader to embrace curiosity as a driving force, pursuing learning and exploration with enthusiasm and commitment.

*Oh Mercury, grant me the art,*
*To share my mind and touch the heart.*
*To adapt, to flex, to stand, to bend,*
*And find the harmony time will send.*

Here, Mercury's energy of adaptability and connection is emphasized. It inspires the reader to balance their intellect with empathy, learning to communicate in ways that resonate with others and foster harmony.

*Through you, I'll rise with steady pace,*
*To meet the world with a nimble grace.*
*A seeker, a thinker, bold and free,*
*Oh Mercury, your strength flows through me.*

The closing stanza empowers the reader to align with Mercury's versatile and dynamic qualities. It encourages them to approach life with boldness, intelligence, and grace, embodying Mercury's strength and adaptability in all they do.

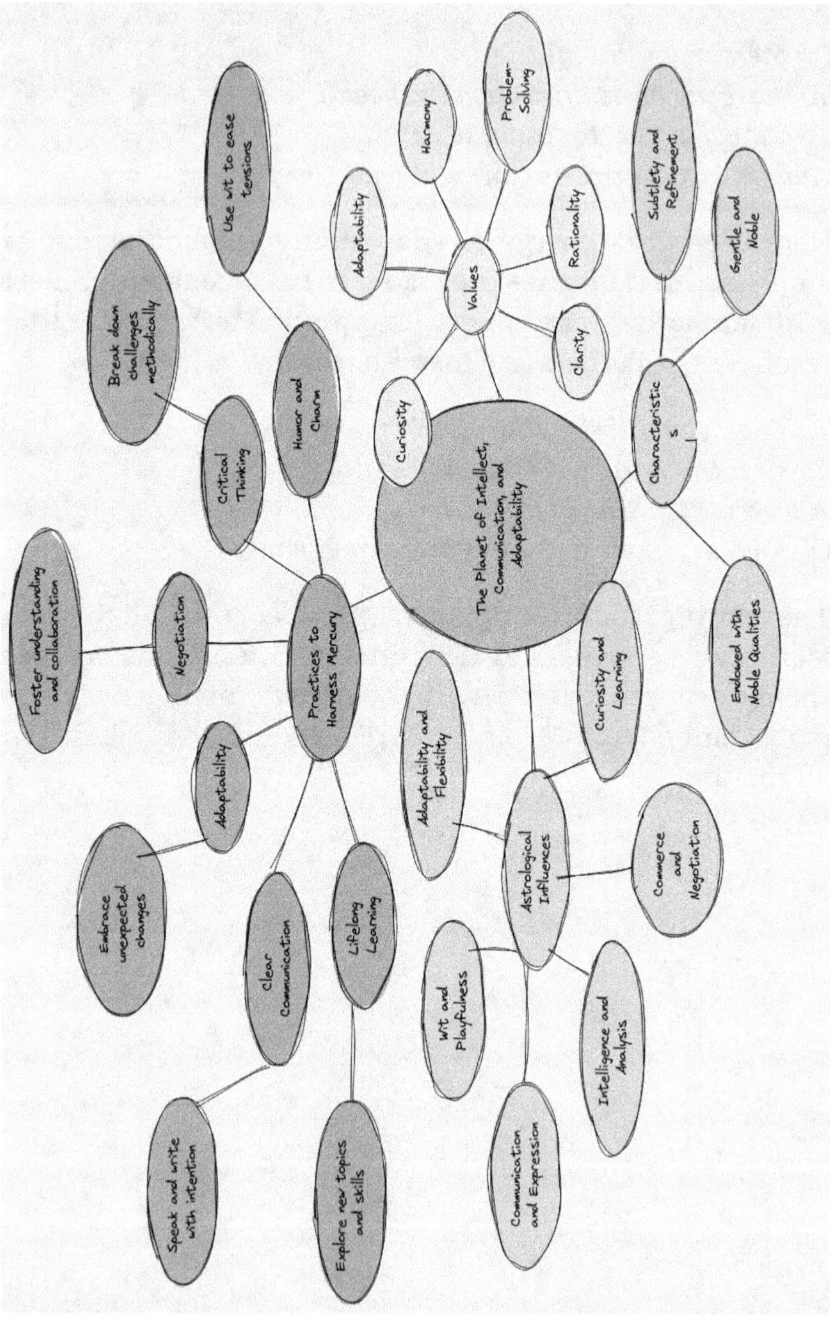
The Planet of Intellect, Communication, and Adaptability
Values
Adaptability
Harmony
Problem-Solving
Rationality
Clarity
Curiosity
Characteristic
s
Subtlety and Refinement
Gentle and Noble
Endowed with Noble Qualities
Curiosity and Learning
Astrological Influences
Adaptability and Flexibility
Commerce and Negotiation
Wit and Playfulness
Intelligence and Analysis
Communication and Expression
Practices to Harness Mercury
Humor and Charm
Use wit to ease tensions
Critical Thinking
Break down challenges methodically
Negotiation
Foster understanding and collaboration
Adaptability
Embrace unexpected changes
Clear Communication
Speak and write with intention
Lifelong Learning
Explore new topics and skills

# JUPITER - THE TEACHER

**Role:** Symbolizes wisdom, spirituality, and expansion.

**Significance:** Jupiter is the planet of knowledge, higher learning, and ethical principles. It represents spiritual guidance and prosperity.

**Associated Aspects:** Teachers, elders, children, wealth, and spiritual growth.

Oh Jupiter, teacher of the stars,
Guide my journey, near and far.
With golden light, so pure, so grand,
Lead me to truths I understand.

You shine with wisdom, vast and deep,
Awake my soul from slumber's sleep.
Through knowledge gained and lessons learned,
Ignite the flame my spirit yearned.

Oh giver of growth, of faith and grace,
Expand my heart, my inner space.
In every challenge, let me find,
A seed of hope to free my mind.

With every word, with every deed,
Show me to serve and meet the need.
Let integrity be my steadfast guide,
With righteousness, let me abide.

Through acts of kindness, bold and true,
I share the gifts received from you.
With open hands, I rise, I give,
In your abundance, I truly live.

Oh Jupiter, Guru divine,
Let your wisdom align with mine.
May I teach, may I inspire,
A torch of truth, a sacred fire.

In your light, I find my way,
With faith that grows, come what may.
A boundless soul, I rise and see,
The endless vastness of destiny.

## Explanation

*Oh Jupiter, teacher of the devas,*
*Guide my journey, near and far.*
*With golden light, so pure, so grand,*
*Lead me to truths I understand.*

This stanza invokes Jupiter's role as a cosmic teacher and guide, symbolizing the light of wisdom and understanding. It encourages the reader to seek clarity and enlightenment, trusting in Jupiter's benevolent energy to illuminate their path.

*You shine with wisdom, vast and deep,*
*Awake my soul from slumber's sleep.*
*Through knowledge gained and lessons learned,*
*Ignite the flame my spirit yearned.*

Here, Jupiter's association with higher learning and spiritual growth is celebrated. It inspires the reader to awaken their inner potential through knowledge and life's lessons, igniting a deep passion for truth and self-discovery.

*Oh giver of growth, of faith and grace,*
*Expand my heart, my inner space.*
*In every challenge, let me find,*
*A seed of hope to free my mind.*

This stanza reflects Jupiter's expansive and optimistic energy. It empowers the reader to embrace challenges as opportunities for growth and to cultivate faith and hope, fostering an open heart and mind.

*With every word, with every deed,*
*Show me to serve and meet the need.*
*Let integrity be my steadfast guide,*
*With righteousness, let me abide.*

Here, Jupiter's dharmic qualities of integrity and moral conduct are emphasized. The reader is encouraged to align their actions with ethical principles and to serve others selflessly, staying true to their higher purpose.

*Through acts of kindness, bold and true,*
*I share the gifts received from you.*
*With open hands, I rise, I give,*
*In your abundance, I truly live.*

This stanza highlights Jupiter's generosity and abundance. It inspires the reader to share their blessings with others, understanding that '*giving*' enriches both the giver and the receiver, creating a life of fulfillment.

*Oh Jupiter, Guru divine,*
*Let your wisdom align with mine.*
*May I teach, may I inspire,*
*A torch of truth, a sacred fire.*

Here, Jupiter's role as a mentor and guide is invoked, encouraging the reader to embody its qualities by teaching and inspiring others. It reflects the transformative power of sharing wisdom and being a beacon of light for others.

*In your light, I find my way,*
*With faith that grows, come what may.*
*A boundless soul, I rise and see,*
*The endless vastness of destiny.*

The closing stanza celebrates Jupiter's expansive energy and the faith it instills. It empowers the reader to rise above limitations, embracing their boundless potential and aligning with the infinite possibilities of their destiny.

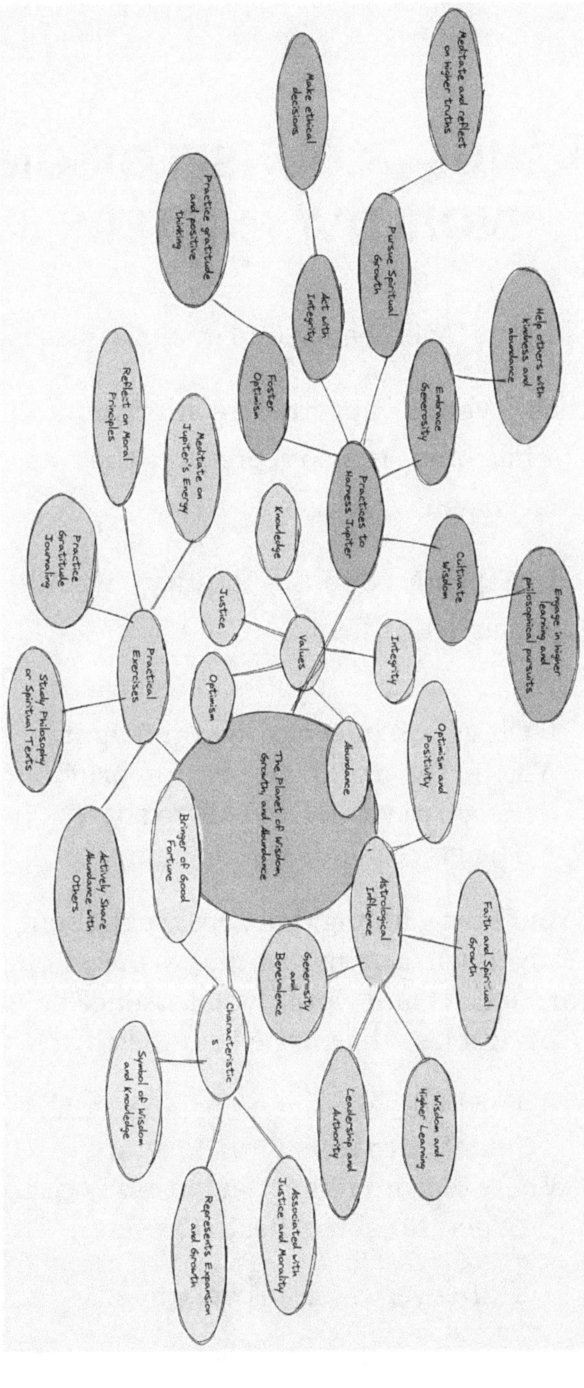
The Planet of Wisdom, Growth, and Abundance
Practices to Harness Jupiter
Cultivate Wisdom
Engage in higher learning and philosophical pursuits
Embrace Generosity
Help others with kindness and abundance
Pursue Spiritual Growth
Meditate and reflect on higher truths
Act with Integrity
Make ethical decisions
Foster Optimism
Practice gratitude and positive thinking
Values
Knowledge
Justice
Integrity
Optimism
Abundance
Practical Exercises
Reflect on Moral Principles
Meditate on Jupiter's Energy
Practice Gratitude Journaling
Study Philosophy or Spiritual Texts
Actively Share Abundance with Others
Optimism and Positivity
Astrological Influence
Faith and Spiritual Growth
Generosity and Benevolence
Wisdom and Higher Learning
Leadership and Authority
Bringer of Good Fortune
Characteristic s
Symbol of Wisdom and Knowledge
Associated with Justice and Morality
Represents Expansion and Growth

# VENUS - COUNSELOR ON WORLDLY MATTERS

**Role:** Represents love, beauty, and material pleasures.

**Significance:** Venus governs relationships, creativity, luxury, and harmony. It also represents the arts, romance, and personal charm.

**Associated Aspects:** Spouse, beauty, wealth, sensual pleasures, and artistic talents.

Oh Venus, queen of love and light,
You fill the world with beauty bright.
Teach me to see, to feel, to share,
The grace in all, beyond compare.

Your voice, a song that soothes the soul,
Your touch, a balm that makes me whole.
Through art and words, your essence flows,
A timeless charm the heart bestows.

Oh bringer of peace, of balance true,
Guide me to walk with poise anew.
Where discord reigns, let harmony rise,
A gentle calm beneath the skies.

In every face, in every hue,

You show the wonder, the pure, the true.
Let my heart embrace with love so kind,
The beauty of life in soul and mind.

Oh Venus, muse of dreams divine,
Inspire the spark, let my spirit shine.
Through acts of care and love sincere,
Let your wisdom draw me near.

In moments of joy, in pleasures found,
May gratitude forever abound.
Through simple gifts or treasures grand,
I cherish life, by your command.

Oh star of compassion, soft and bright,
You heal the heart, you bring delight.
Let me embody your gentle art,
To spread your grace in every part.

With Venus as guide, my soul will rise,
A beacon of love beneath the skies.
Through beauty, balance, and care profound,
I'll weave your magic all around.

## Explanation

*Oh Venus, queen of love and light,*
*You fill the world with beauty bright.*
*Teach me to see, to feel, to share,*
*The grace in all, beyond compare.*

This stanza honors Venus as the embodiment of love, light, and beauty, inspiring the reader to cultivate awareness of the elegance and harmony in life. It calls for opening the heart to appreciate and share the grace that surrounds us.

*Your voice, a song that soothes the soul,*
*Your touch, a balm that makes me whole.*
*Through art and words, your essence flows,*
*A timeless charm the heart bestows.*

*Shukracharya* (Venus) the teacher of the demons was also a wise healer and considered to have the knowledge of brining back someone even from the jaws of death. Here, Venus is depicted as a source of healing and inspiration. The stanza encourages the reader to express themselves creatively and recognize the healing power of art and words in connecting with their inner self and others.

*Oh bringer of peace, of balance true,*
*Guide me to walk with poise anew.*
*Where discord reigns, let harmony rise,*
*A gentle calm beneath the skies.*

This stanza emphasizes Venus' role in fostering balance and harmony. It inspires the reader to become a force of peace, learning to navigate conflicts with grace and bringing equilibrium to their relationships and surroundings.

*In every face, in every hue,*
*You show the wonder, the pure, the true.*
*Let my heart embrace with love so kind,*
*The beauty of life in soul and mind.*

Venus' energy of universal love is celebrated here, urging the reader to see beauty and purity in everyone and everything. It empowers them to cultivate kindness and love that transcends superficial differences.

*Oh Venus, muse of dreams divine,*
*Inspire the spark, let my spirit shine.*
*Through acts of care and love sincere,*
*Let your wisdom draw me near.*

This stanza invokes Venus as the source of inspiration and light, encouraging the reader to embody love and compassion in their actions. It reflects the transformative power of sincere care in building meaningful connections.

*In moments of joy, in pleasures found,*
*May gratitude forever abound.*
*Through simple gifts or treasures grand,*
*I cherish life, by your command.*

Here, Venus' association with abundance and gratitude is highlighted. The stanza inspires the reader to appreciate life's blessings, big or small, and to nurture a mindset of gratitude for the richness of existence.

*Oh star of compassion, soft and bright,*
*You heal the heart, you bring delight.*
*Let me embody your gentle art,*
*To spread your grace in every part.*

This stanza reinforces Venus' role as a healer and guide, encouraging the reader to embody compassion and bring joy to others. It serves as a reminder to channel Venus' energy through acts of kindness and empathy.

*With Venus as guide, my soul will rise,*
*A beacon of love beneath the skies.*
*Through beauty, balance, and care profound,*
*I'll weave your magic all around.*

The final stanza empowers the reader to live as a reflection of Venus' qualities—love, balance, and beauty. It inspires them to rise as a source of light and grace, spreading Venus' energy to create a life filled with harmony and joy.

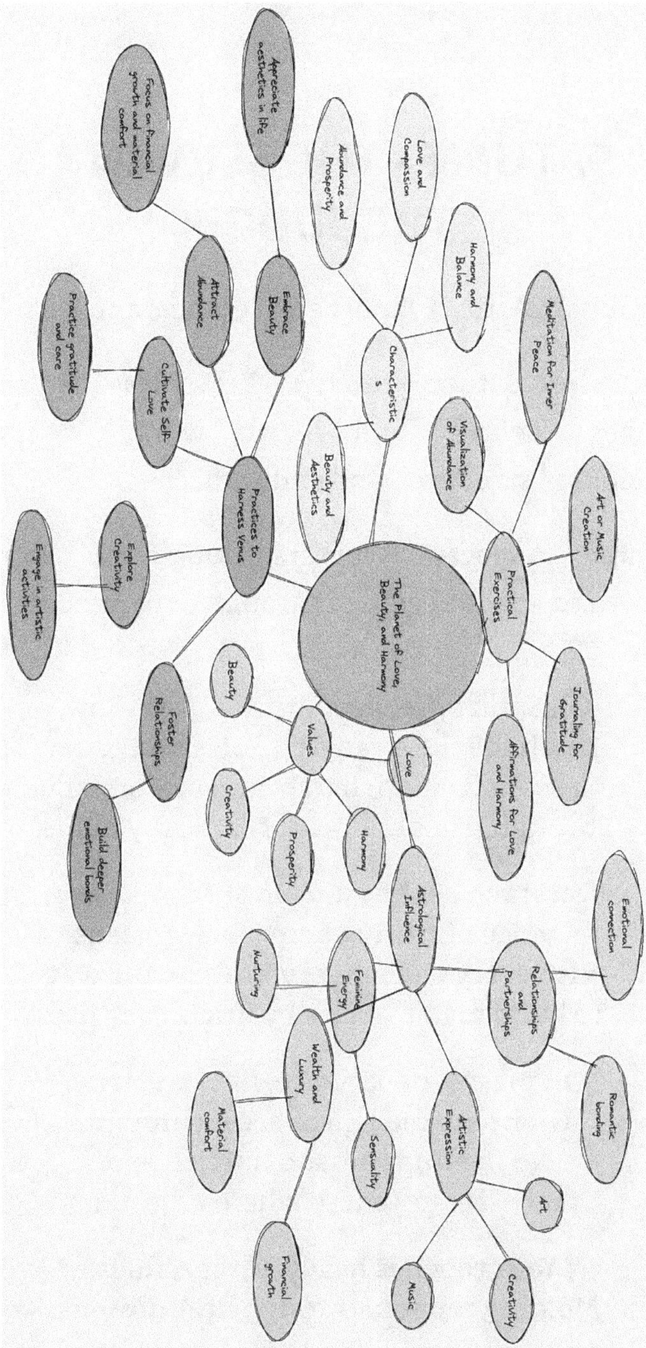
The Planet of Love, Beauty, and Harmony
Characteristics
Love and Compassion
Abundance and Prosperity
Harmony and Balance
Beauty and Aesthetics
Practices to Harness Venus
Embrace Beauty
Appreciate aesthetics in life
Attract Abundance
Focus on financial growth and material comfort
Cultivate Self Love
Practice gratitude and care
Explore Creativity
Engage in artistic activities
Foster Relationships
Build deeper emotional bonds
Values
Beauty
Love
Creativity
Prosperity
Harmony
Practical Exercises
Meditation for Inner Peace
Visualization of Abundance
Art or Music Creation
Journaling for Gratitude
Affirmations for Love and Harmony
Astrological Influence
Feminine Energy
Nurturing
Sensuality
Wealth and Luxury
Material comfort
Financial growth
Relationships and Partnerships
Emotional connection
Romantic bonding
Artistic Expression
Art
Music
Creativity

# SATURN - THE SERVANT , THE JUDGE

**Role:** Symbolizes discipline, perseverance, and karma.

**Significance:** Saturn teaches life's lessons through challenges, delays, and hard work. It governs responsibility, structure, and endurance.

**Associated Aspects:** Workers, longevity, hardships, patience, and wisdom gained through experience.

Oh Saturn, keeper of time's great flow,
Teach me the strength to rise and grow.
Your lessons, though harsh, are wisdom's flame,
Through trials endured, I carve my name.

You stand as the guide in shadows deep,
A voice of truth where silence sleeps.
With every challenge, you show the way,
To build my life, brick by brick, each day.

Oh master of patience, firm and true,
Grant me the will to see it through.
No fleeting gain, no hurried end,
But a steady climb where I ascend.

Your touch is heavy, yet it refines,
Molding my soul through life's designs.

Through discipline's hand, my power grows,
In struggle's forge, resilience shows.

Oh bringer of justice, fair and right,
Guide my steps with moral light.
Let me stand tall with truth as my shield,
On the battleground where courage is revealed.

Through shadows long, I find my ground,
In every fall, your strength is found.
With humility's grace, I rise once more,
A stronger soul than ever before.

Oh Saturn, lord of endurance and fate,
Teach me to master life's heavy weight.
For in your wisdom, I learn to strive,
Through patience and will, I truly thrive.

In your lessons, I see the way,
To build a life that will not sway.
A legacy strong, both just and wise,
Oh Saturn, my guide beneath the skies.

## Explanation

*Oh Saturn, keeper of time's great flow,*
*Teach me the strength to rise and grow.*
*Your lessons, though harsh, are wisdom's flame,*
*Through trials endured, I carve my name.*

This stanza introduces Saturn as the teacher of time and endurance. It acknowledges that while Saturn's lessons are challenging, they are the source of growth and strength. It empowers the reader to embrace hardships as opportunities to forge a resilient identity.

*You stand as the guide in shadows deep,*
*A voice of truth where silence sleeps.*
*With every challenge, you show the way,*
*To build my life, brick by brick, each day.*

Here, Saturn is depicted as a guide through life's darker and quieter moments, encouraging the reader to find clarity and purpose amidst struggles. The stanza emphasizes patience and steady effort in creating a strong and lasting foundation for life.

*Oh master of patience, firm and true,*
*Grant me the will to see it through.*
*No fleeting gain, no hurried end,*
*But a steady climb where I ascend.*

This stanza highlights Saturn's emphasis on patience and perseverance. It inspires the reader to resist the lure of quick fixes and instead focus on gradual, meaningful progress, fostering a sense of commitment to long-term goals.

*Your touch is heavy, yet it refines,*
*Molding my soul through life's designs.*
*Through discipline's hand, my power grows,*
*In struggle's forge, resilience shows.*

Saturn's transformative energy is celebrated here as a force that shapes the soul through discipline and endurance. It reminds the reader that challenges are opportunities to grow stronger and wiser, refining their character through persistence.

*Oh bringer of justice, fair and right,*
*Guide my steps with moral light.*
*Let me stand tall with truth as my shield,*
*On the battleground where courage is revealed.*

This stanza reflects Saturn's role as the arbiter of karma and justice. It encourages the reader to act with integrity, using truth as a guiding principle in overcoming life's obstacles and standing firm in the face of adversity.

*Through shadows long, I find my ground,*
*In every fall, your strength is found.*
*With humility's grace, I rise once more,*
*A stronger soul than ever before.*

Here, the poem acknowledges that setbacks and failures are part of Saturn's lessons. It empowers the reader to rise after every fall, embracing humility as a path to greater strength and self-awareness.

*Oh Saturn, lord of endurance and fate,*
*Teach me to master life's heavy weight.*
*For in your wisdom, I learn to strive,*
*Through patience and will, I truly thrive.*

This stanza calls on Saturn's wisdom to help the reader embrace life's burdens with grace. It inspires them to strive with patience and determination, recognizing that perseverance leads to true fulfillment.

*In your lessons, I see the way,*
*To build a life that will not sway.*
*A legacy strong, both just and wise,*
*Oh Saturn, my guide beneath the skies.*

The closing stanza celebrates Saturn's teachings as the foundation for building a meaningful and enduring life. It urges the reader to embrace the discipline and integrity needed to leave a lasting legacy of strength and wisdom.

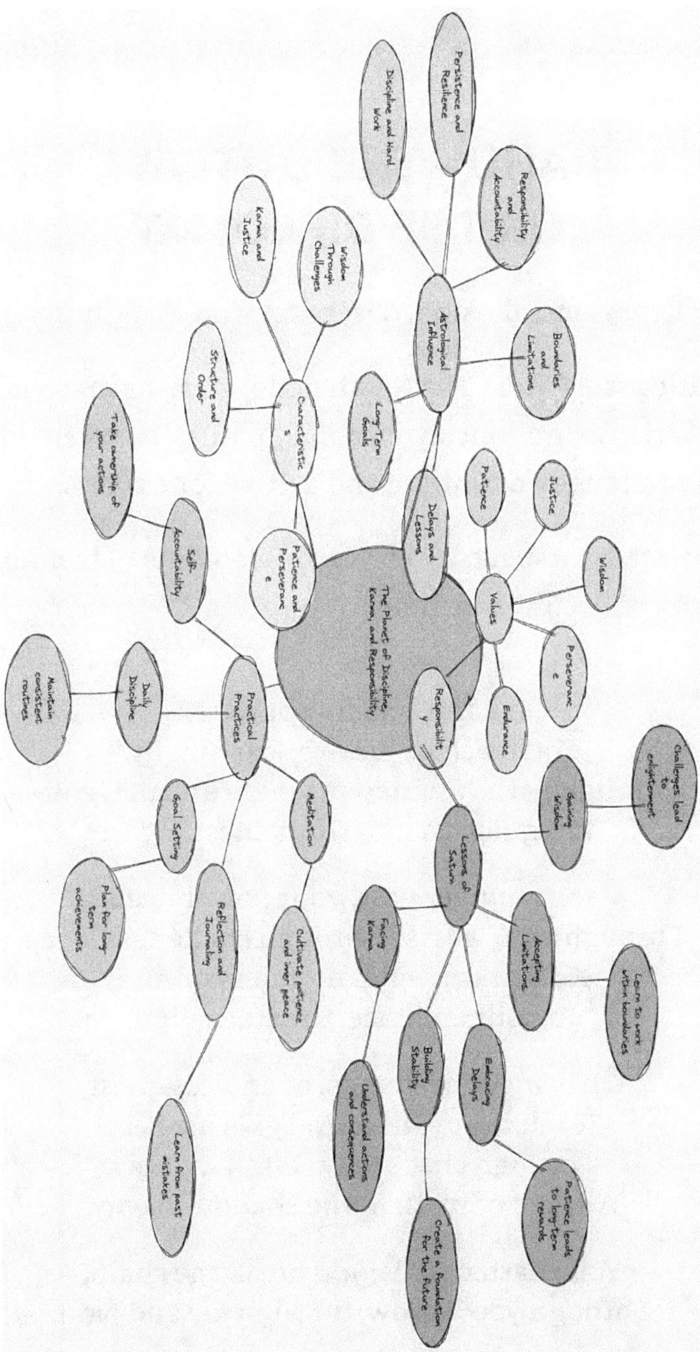
The Planet of Discipline, Karma, and Responsibility
Characteristics
Structure and Order
Karma and Justice
Wisdom Through Challenges
Patience and Perseverance
Astrological Influence
Discipline and Hard Work
Persistence and Resilience
Responsibility and Accountability
Boundaries and Limitations
Long Term Goals
Delays and Lessons
Values
Patience
Justice
Wisdom
Perseverance
Endurance
Responsibility
Lessons of Saturn
Gaining Wisdom
Challenges lead to enlightenment
Facing Karma
Understand actions and consequences
Accepting Limitations
Learn to work within boundaries
Embracing Delays
Patience leads to long-term rewards
Building Stability
Create a Foundation for the Future
Practical Practices
Self-Accountability
Take ownership of your actions
Daily Discipline
Maintain consistent routines
Goal Setting
Plan for long term achievements
Meditation
Cultivate patience and inner peace
Reflection and Journaling
Learn from past mistakes

# RAHU - THE OUTLAW, OR THE DIPLOMAT

**Role:** Represents illusion, obsession, and worldly desires.

**Significance:** Rahu ( The North node) governs materialism, innovation, and unconventional paths. It often brings sudden changes, ambition, and a drive for success.

**Associated Aspects:** Foreign elements, technology, deception, occult, and fame.

Oh Rahu, shadow of the sky,
You teach us how to soar and fly.
Through paths unknown, where dreams ignite,
You guide us into the boldest night.

Your hunger vast, your power deep,
Through you, we rise, through challenges steep.
No fear can bind, no rules confine,
In your embrace, the stars align.

Oh bringer of change, of endless quest,
Teach me to strive and give my best.
Through chaos dark, I find my way,
A spark of truth in the shadow's sway.

You shatter walls, you break the chain,
Through you, I grow, through joy and pain.

Each step I take, a fearless stride,
With you, I learn to turn the tide.

Oh master of bold and restless desire,
Fuel my heart with your boundless fire.
Let ambition rise, let courage grow,
Through Rahu's energy, the unknown I'll know.

Through illusions vast, let clarity shine,
Through trials hard, let strength be mine.
Oh Rahu, show me what's unseen,
To claim the life I've always dreamed.

In shadows cast, I see the light,
In chaos, I find my inner might.
With Rahu as guide, I dare to be,
A force of change, bold and free.

## Explanation

*Oh Rahu, shadow of the sky,*
*You teach us how to soar and fly.*
*Through paths unknown, where dreams ignite,*
*You guide us into the boldest night.*

This stanza introduces Rahu as a force of ambition and exploration, encouraging the reader to step into the unknown with courage. It emphasizes Rahu's role in awakening bold dreams and pushing boundaries, inspiring a fearless pursuit of aspirations.

*Your hunger vast, your power deep,*
*Through you, we rise, through challenges steep.*
*No fear can bind, no rules confine,*

*In your embrace, the stars align.*

Here, Rahu's limitless energy and transformative power are celebrated. It inspires the reader to rise above fear and limitations, trusting that Rahu's guidance aligns their efforts with a greater purpose, even amidst challenges.

*Oh bringer of change, of endless quest,*
*Teach me to strive and give my best.*
*Through chaos dark, I find my way,*
*A spark of truth in the shadow's sway.*

This stanza highlights Rahu's connection to transformation through chaos. It empowers the reader to embrace change and strive for excellence, using challenges as opportunities to uncover deeper truths and forge a meaningful path.

*You shatter walls, you break the chain,*
*Through you, I grow, through joy and pain.*
*Each step I take, a fearless stride,*
*With you, I learn to turn the tide.*

Here, Rahu's ability to disrupt and liberate is acknowledged. The stanza encourages the reader to break free from constraints and use both joy and pain as catalysts for growth. It inspires bold, fearless actions to overcome obstacles and create change.

*Oh master of bold and restless desire,*
*Fuel my heart with your boundless fire.*
*Let ambition rise, let courage grow,*
*Through Rahu's energy, the unknown I'll know.*

This stanza invokes Rahu's restless and ambitious energy,

urging the reader to harness its fire to fuel courage and curiosity. It inspires a willingness to embrace the unknown and pursue ambitious goals with determination.

*Through illusions vast, let clarity shine,*
*Through trials hard, let strength be mine.*
*Oh Rahu, show me what's unseen,*
*To claim the life I've always dreamed.*

Here, Rahu's association with illusion and clarity is explored. The stanza empowers the reader to move beyond distractions and gain insight, transforming trials into strength and uncovering hidden potential to achieve their dreams.

*In shadows cast, I see the light,*
*In chaos, I find my inner might.*
*With Rahu as guide, I dare to be,*
*A force of change, bold and free.*

The closing stanza celebrates Rahu as a guide through life's uncertainties. It encourages the reader to find strength within chaos, embodying courage and becoming a transformative force in their own life. It inspires freedom through self-discovery and bold action.

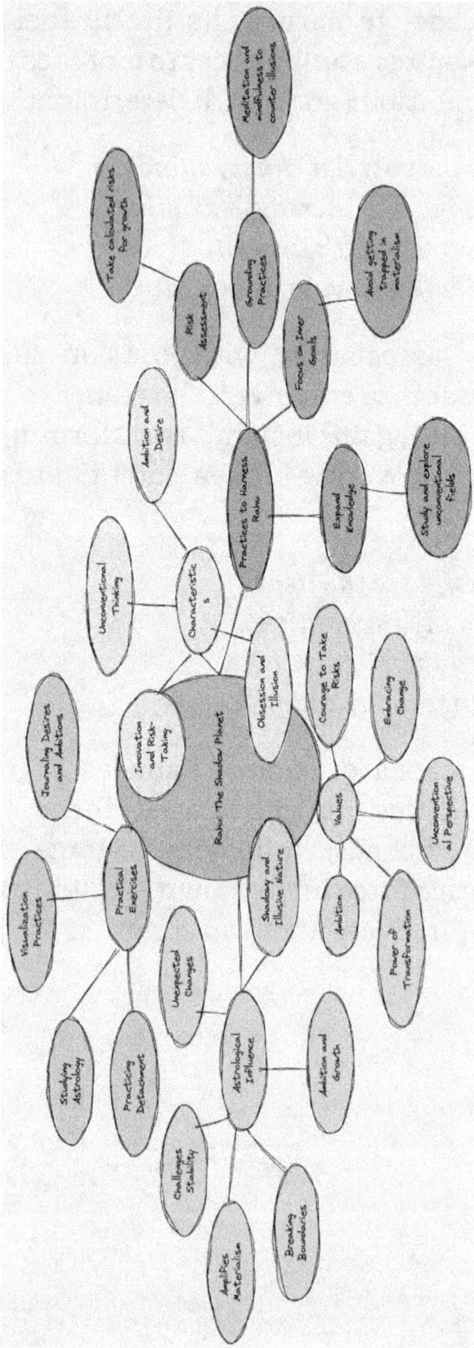
Rahu: The Shadow Planet
Innovation and Risk-Taking
Obsession and Illusion
Characteristic s
Unconventional Thinking
Ambition and Desire
Practices to Harness Rahu
Risk Assessment
Take calculated risks for growth
Grounding Practices
Meditation and mindfulness to counter illusions
Focus on Inner Goals
Avoid getting trapped in materialism
Expand Knowledge
Study and explore unconventional fields
Courage to Take Risks
Embracing Change
Values
Unconvention al Perspective
Ambition
Power of Transformation
Shadowy and Illusive Nature
Journaling Desires and Ambitions
Practical Exercises
Visualization Practices
Studying Astrology
Practicing Detachment
Unexpected Changes
Astrological Influence
Ambition and Growth
Challenges Stability
Amplifies Materialism
Breaking Boundaries

# KETU - THE MYSTIC , THE SAGE

**Role:** Symbolizes detachment, spirituality, and liberation.
**Significance:** Ketu (The South node) is associated with past-life karma, spiritual growth, and transcendence. It encourages detachment from material desires.
**Associated Aspects:** Moksha (liberation), all sorts of ancient sciences, intuition, and introspection.

Oh Ketu, shadow of the soul,
You break the chains that make us whole.
With every bond that fades away,
You guide us to a brighter day.

Your touch is fierce, your wisdom pure,
Through you, we learn what will endure.
No fleeting riches, no hollow pride,
Just truth and peace, where joy resides.

Oh master of silence, calm and still,
Teach me the strength of a quiet will.
To let things go, to seek within,
The boundless light where life begins.

Through wounds of past and shadows deep,
You heal the scars we choose to keep.
In every loss, a gift is found,
A soul unchained, a life unbound.

Oh seeker of truths, unseen, unknown,
Through you, the seeds of wisdom are sown.
Your mystic touch, your guiding flame,
Transforms the self, removes the blame.

Through simple joys and paths austere,
You show the way to a life sincere.
No weight of ego, no need for more,
Through Ketu's grace, the spirit soars.

Oh star of detachment, soft yet strong,
You teach what's right, not what's wrong.
With Ketu's power, I rise, I see,
The beauty of life's simplicity.

In shadows deep, I find my peace,
Through Ketu's light, my burdens cease.
With every step, I walk the line,
To liberation's truth divine.

## Explanation

*Oh Ketu, shadow of the soul,*
*You break the chains that make us whole.*
*With every bond that fades away,*
*You guide us to a brighter day.*

This stanza introduces Ketu as the force that liberates the soul by breaking attachments. It empowers the reader to let go of limiting bonds and embrace the clarity and light that come from freedom and detachment.

*Your touch is fierce, your wisdom pure,*
*Through you, we learn what will endure.*

*No fleeting riches, no hollow pride,*
*Just truth and peace, where joy resides.*

Here, Ketu's transformative and introspective nature is highlighted. The stanza encourages the reader to focus on enduring truths rather than transient material pursuits, finding lasting joy in simplicity and authenticity.

*Oh master of silence, calm and still,*
*Teach me the strength of a quiet will.*
*To let things go, to seek within,*
*The boundless light where life begins.*

This stanza emphasizes Ketu's connection to inner peace and spiritual strength. It inspires the reader to cultivate stillness, look inward, and access the infinite light of self-awareness and spiritual growth.

*Through wounds of past and shadows deep,*
*You heal the scars we choose to keep.*
*In every loss, a gift is found,*
*A soul unchained, a life unbound.*

Ketu's healing energy ( healing through decay of old and transformation in to new) is explored here, showing how pain and loss can lead to transformation and liberation. It empowers the reader to release past wounds, seeing them as opportunities to grow and live freely.

*Oh seeker of truths, unseen, unknown,*
*Through you, the seeds of wisdom are sown.*
*Your mystic touch, your guiding flame,*
*Transforms the self, removes the blame.*

This stanza celebrates Ketu's role as a seeker of higher

truths and inner wisdom. It encourages the reader to embrace self-transformation, shedding blame and ego to uncover deeper understanding and purpose.

*Through simple joys and paths austere,*
*You show the way to a life sincere.*
*No weight of ego, no need for more,*
*Through Ketu's grace, the spirit soars.*

Here, Ketu's lesson of simplicity and humility is reflected. The stanza inspires the reader to find fulfillment in a life free from ego and material excess, aligning with their truest self.

*Oh star of detachment, soft yet strong,*
*You teach what's right, not what's wrong.*
*With Ketu's power, I rise, I see,*
*The beauty of life's simplicity.*

This stanza acknowledges Ketu's gentle yet profound influence, guiding the reader toward wisdom and simplicity. It encourages embracing detachment as a path to inner peace and clarity.

*In shadows deep, I find my peace,*
*Through Ketu's light, my burdens cease.*
*With every step, I walk the line,*
*To liberation's truth divine.*

The closing stanza reinforces Ketu's role in helping the reader find peace in the depths of life's challenges. It inspires a journey of liberation and spiritual awakening, walking a path guided by Ketu's transformative light.

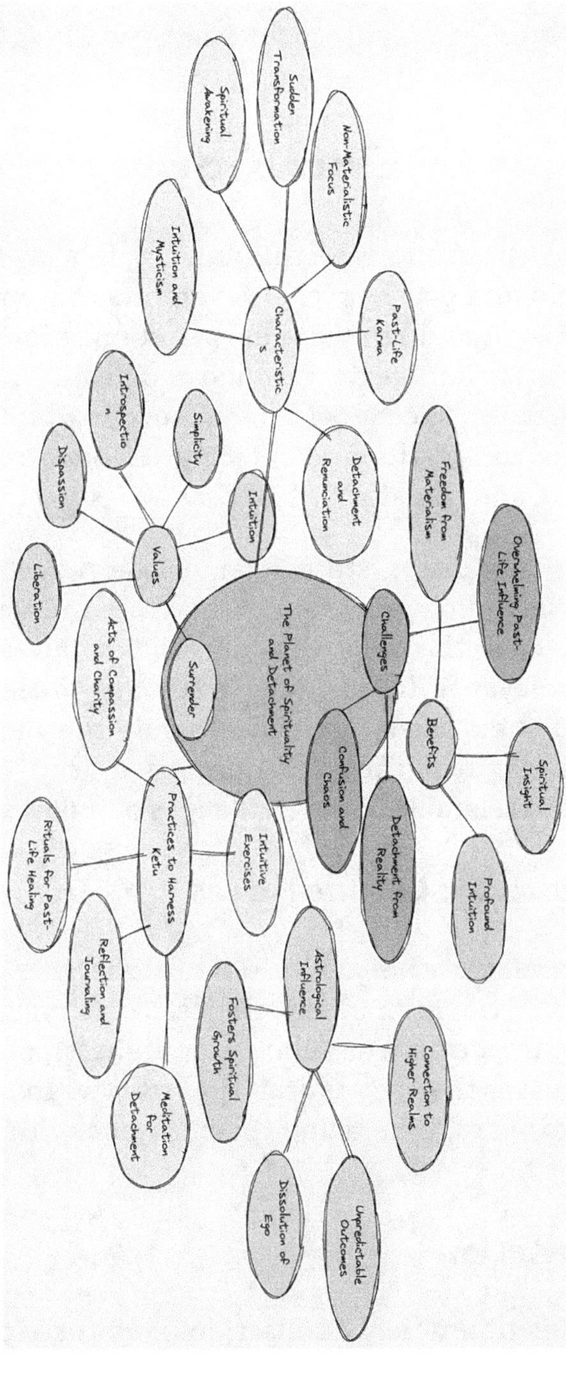
The Planet of Spirituality and Detachment
Characteristic s
Sudden Transformation
Spiritual Awakening
Non-Materialistic Focus
Intuition and Mysticism
Past-Life Karma
Detachment and Renunciation
Values
Introspectio n
Simplicity
Dispassion
Intuition
Liberation
Surrender
Acts of Compassion and Charity
Challenges
Freedom from Materialism
Overwhelming Past-Life Influence
Confusion and Chaos
Detachment from Reality
Benefits
Spiritual Insight
Profound Intuition
Practices to Harness Ketu
Intuitive Exercises
Rituals for Past-Life Healing
Reflection and Journaling
Meditation for Detachment
Astrological Influence
Fosters Spiritual Growth
Connection to Higher Realms
Dissolution of Ego
Unpredictable Outcomes

# EPILOGUE

As we draw the curtains on this journey, it is my hope that the wisdom and poetry of the **Navagrahas** have resonated with your soul and ignited a deeper connection with the cosmic forces that weave through our lives. The planets are not distant spectators; they are dynamic energies, influencing our paths and offering us opportunities to grow, learn, and transform.

Through the mantras, stotras, and modern poetry in this book, we have explored not only the profound astrological significance of the nine celestial bodies but also their timeless relevance to our daily lives. The ancient verses whispered their sacred guidance, while the modern-day poetry reimagined their energies in a way that feels tangible and relatable to the challenges of today.

## Living with the Cosmic Forces

The Navagrahas are not just deities or archetypes—they are reflections of the human experience. Their cycles remind us of life's impermanence and its boundless potential for renewal. Just as the planets orbit tirelessly, we too are called to move forward, embracing their lessons with humility and strength.

## A Call to Action

This book is not merely a collection of words—it is a tool,

a companion, and a guide. Use the mantras as a starting point to attune yourself to the planets' vibrations. Reflect on the poetry to find meaning in their movements. Allow their energies in conjunction with Karmic initiatives to shape your actions, your relationships, and your path toward self-discovery.

*May all beings be happy !*

# ABOUT THE AUTHOR

## Nitin Vasishtha

Born in Varanasi into a lineage of spiritual seekers, Nitin Vasishtha's journey ventured far beyond tradition. Armed with degrees in engineering and business, he climbed the corporate ladder and experienced the peaks and valleys of entrepreneurship, uncovering a profound truth: no one is at complete peace. Everyone, in their own way, is grappling with the urge to change something about their lives—striving to fix, achieve, or become.

Since 1996, Nitin has immersed himself in astrology, spirituality, and human psychology, decoding life's complexities and using these ancient tools to guide himself and helping others reflect on their personal journeys.

As a life-purpose and relationship counselor, CrossFit enthusiast, Ultra- marathon runner, and biohacker, Nitin bridges the gap between ancient wisdom and modern living.

Through relatable poems, storytelling and actionable insights, he encourages readers to rethink their paths, embrace their struggles, and find clarity amidst life's chaos. When he's not writing or engaging with curious minds, you'll find him playing with his dog, Yaara, or unraveling the intersections of self-awareness, free will, and the human spirit. Nitin currently resides in Bangalore, India.

www.ingramcontent.com/pod-product-compliance
Lightning Source LLC
Chambersburg PA
CBHW062144160726
48282CB00027B/935